D0796960

Of Being Dispersed

FUTUREPOEM BOOKS
NEW YORK CITY

Of Being Dispersed

Simone White

Copyright © 2016 Simone White
ISBN: 978-0-9960025-4-7

First published in 2016 by Futurepoem books
P.O. Box 7687 JAF Station, NY, NY 10116
www.futurepoem.com
Third printing 2020.

Executive Editor: Dan Machlin
Managing Editor: Carly Dashiell
Books Editor: Ted Dodson
Guest Editors: Myung Mi Kim, Albert Mobilio, and Ben Lerner

Cover design: Everything Studio (www.everythingstudio.com)
Interior design: HR Hegnauer (www.hrhegnauer.com)
Typeface: Minion
Printed in the United States of America on acid-free paper

This project is supported in part by the New York State Council on the Arts with the
support of Governor Andrew Cuomo and the New York State Legislature, as well as
by The Leaves of Grass Fund, The New York Community Trust and our individual
supporters and subscribers. Futurepoem books is the publishing program of
Futurepoem, Inc., a New York state-based 501(c)3 non-profit organization dedicated
to creating a greater public awareness and appreciation of innovative literature.

Distributed to the trade by Small Press Distribution, Berkeley, California
Toll-free number (U.S. only): 800.869.7553
Bay Area/International: 510.524.1668
orders@spdbooks.org
www.spdbooks.org

sister, brother, husband

Then I began to hear the call of Los Angeles.
The best rooms in the apartment faced North.
My husband tried to put me where I could entertain
winter light, the lavender paint-idea, the sectional
porn poured in from design blogs. Well,
it was no use. Los Angeles was on my face;

it was hot and harmless.
Before I burned up and rolled away,
black-ass tumbleweed, as had happened so many times
in dreams that year, it was important that I get there
or get some information my papa was trying to get across,
like, GO TO LOS ANGELES

(where dead negroes can't get in your house).
Yeah.
It has been suggested that I am insufficiently open
to the possible presence of occult phenomena
on this earth. Voices of the dead, which I just told you
come around/irritate me, rock kinetics,

shamans and people who clear auras,
I do not deal in. Not because they are not real,
but because they are, I do not deal in them.
Los Angeles of the hidden garden, of the carved-up
starlet, acres of strange dick, items
of unclear provenance and arbitrary value.

There is a hotel in West Hollywood, quite near
the bungalow of an old friend who can make shoes
out of wood and boiled wool, but that is just
an example of what she can do. I would like
to take a room in this hotel for weeks on end
and pretend to be dead. I should drink champagne

and refuse help, then move to another hotel. Perhaps,
the Beverly Hills.

Comment

'Avant le circonflexe, on a cru que tous l'écriture etait écrit dans la langue du réflexion. Thus, the language I learned to speak at birth comments upon relative inscription.'

Commentary, first mode of elaboration, before inquiry, people just rapping in caves.

In feelings of and for total loss, the fullness of maturity mauled and harassed me. In my marriage and with my mother, there was truly no celebration of my imaginary self, still caterwauling in the way-behind.

The subways could be anywhere because a state of unhearingness prevails there; unless there is an emergency, and people begin to speak.

From the Old French *comment* and before that the Latin for "invention, contrivance, enthymeme." Speech from or with *mens*: Speech that has wishes, wishing to be more than sound; that non-talk for which the poetic so painfully hopes.

Also, commend. I commend to you a period of abstinence. Preferably from drink. I eked out the most moderate drunkenness for many lonely days. I poured thimblefuls of white wine and still staggered under the same motherfucker of a headache. My liver was tender, very tender. I wanted to say, "The principle of this body is to put out. Invagination is a cosmic scam!"

You have a complicated way of speaking.

This chicken store was not yet operational. Its nice grey sign attempted a ridiculous balance between [come hither] and [it doesn't so much matter whether you come or not]. I know what a chicken is, though. What is that talent called, with fonts? Because fried chicken is a wholesome snack, I command you:

Get outta here, nigga! Kiss my black ass! "Discours qui font rire."

Hot Bird. Hot Bird. Hot Bird. Every few miles on the circuit: one need not starve to death this evening. Lemon yellow and red, yolk and hen, rolled in red dirt.

My relationship to chicken is uncomplicated.

Your sentences trail off into muttering when your nerves get the better of you. Your thigh becomes frantic, your palm presses down on it as if in secret, but everyone can see your thigh, which is not connected to your palm but to your hip and the ball of your foot. Eyeballs, tongue, your whole leg kicks out against the piece you would say. I see how patience is a kind of caress. Let history be borne out in stutters, in mania and grappling.

Awash in delay forever, I had wished for it, and made it so. What was true was also filthy, was surgical. I had the fingers for it.

8

Of Being Dispersed

Waters

as it were in the blood

availed of ability to ride

it could be on horseback the way you appear most
regular

not to be ridden   I understand

the necessarily imagined whip

burdens banging against both flanks   your loose

neglected mad horse someone eventually shoots

in the name of most gentle barbarity

what a terrible swimmer you were

now your son is no swimmer dude seriously

many times his little body was stuck on me

a barnacle   or hung little albatross

apologize never
and always claw my back

waters roll off me

they ride me or I ride them   it is a complexity

whether one is being

done for or doing in your element

Pestilent

Whereabouts   my brother   somewhere

in night sweat

pestilent learnèd most inside of inside?

Whereabouts his manner   having disappeared

returns awash.

Never and always my brother

renews twoness   ungendered forms
uninterviewed.

:   Ocean Parkway and what?
:   The bar there, it takes my dog Wrath.
:   Riff or to float you?
:   W-R-A-T-H. Duh.

:   My Honeymoon.
       The Surfers.

:   Turpentine won't erase your greasy hopes
:   or daily refusal to stand up on the sea.
      Impossibility is for drunks.
:   Stand up! Stand up on the sea.
:   Just this morning hundreds, barefoot, rose,
:   to walk on water as testimony.
:   Our will to grip and destroy the physical laws;
:   it is the essence of navigation,
:   also of not drowning. You are so deeply lazy.
:   Everyone makes me work ungodly
:   hard to keep him with me.

Metaphor for the
Changing Season

All I was thinking or would ever think was happening in a closet.
I could never be joined there by anyone but you. You and you
and I were all there was. The enfolding thing, to pulsate. Parts
broke off and spun away. We were capsular or corpuscular in
terms both of destiny and lack of destination. Parts broke off and
I looked to you to see if thoughts had been had by anybody.

:   Can I meet you at Supreme?

:

:   I can't meet you at Supreme?

:   I can work the subway and meet you at Supreme.

Actionary

Who can give   an account of occasions

Can   mechanized description so falter

Can move toward gesture to scissor the outline

Each to enable a series of seconds   breaking or burning

Can undo the work of a million years   of human love

if I curse you just right

Song Cave

I say an imprint of bones

inked-up   at the bottom of the body

someone complains of barrenness

she is spread apart   marks the progress of   feminine disease

echolocate why don't you joints of foot

and ankle which

bend the knee which

creaks   does your pelvis sigh   also

to bend

press your black fanning bones into fabric   receive an evidence

entire and open   of hinge,

so as not to embarrass my comrades   I suppress an encounter with the grand
domestic fantasy of loft living   on the vestigial tail of Queens   up five stories
slatted blinds   rebuke the ideal life one thinks   one is living in the trash stream

oh a patch of lawn   if that is this   municipal rug of blade and clod   laid-by
carelessly

late-Robert Moses assails us with so many new objects   one thinks   oh a crescent
moon   and it is nothing but onramp   beheld improperly

many thousands of feathers   known to me only as the feathers of a quill pen   more
likely   that image of feather   on Litia's forearm germinates
to become also the pattern of feathers on silk leggings we admire

these feathers   I have hung on the white van of our progressive imagination   have
made myself   a driverless totem   let us not then parade barf-bag wisdoms

disrespecting our vision like that

only to discover a previous triangulation error had led away after all
from restful hormone vacation   that in the dollar van was only lust
for I was between the naked thighs of a middle-aged star of the silver screen
towed in the wake of his walking   where I confirmed the athletic socks he wore
as in fact synthetic   such as are necessary
for serious work

my sister was a blue goddess bureaucrat   whose strict standard governed our intricate
course   patterned movements unapproved by her were halted   I felt my
husband's hand
on my knee   only to become   doubly paranoid

clearly the screw was me   but the jaws were multiple   more at least than two
I dangled lonely in the van   beneath the scrotum of Jeff Daniels

it is the cause my soul

insurgent voltage shot through me at some depth   like the charge of an egg dropt
you have the feel for it so much   in its power you grow stupider until who knows when
I am so tired

Lord of these pains   call me a woman to brush me all over   rest me
from any who would take my blood   even though

I put my vein out like a ho

Its Principal Theorist

Palsy filled up my view of what happened
not of ease where there is no ease
how best to defend the soft limb
shorn vertebrae oh to fold and fall down
on rich baby sweatpants

Windrim

To Windrim or sycamore
      rustle cicada or bark and to Wayne
      to rustle and psoas and psoas to Belmont and Germantown hills
hills as to nearer Plateau as to Central and whisper wall Indian
summer to sleeves or the sleeveless groin as to forward
and dog shit and Cliveden to Wieland the whispering creek
as to Windrim
or mounting as Chestnut to backslid
the Juniper Schuylkill
      to boulder the pound to clover mite
vernal or rake as to tendon
exhaust of to Windrim and spare Wissahickon
of interval granite of peppers of salt-meat of bread
viney cicada   of futures and snowdrift and headlit black sycamore
      peel as to epic and Eakins to whisper to row
      and rape and Windrim to six and of rape and of rocks and of East
the Ursa the middle or buckle and Olney
      of hat
as stone   circuit to Windrim or edge as to pace
as to vise   the falls

Some Creek

One ear to this singing black boulder, lipping
a gravitational problem way more serious
when autumn's considered essentially fallen
a collapsed situation, the bodies all scrambling up rocks
absent whole sides of themselves
they had left on the ground, so heaving

grotesque hulks that trailed seeds that made the lips black
thus reminded of products of miscegenation, that's spring
though, one day to climb up and break
that wretched Indian statue in the woods
the want of true granite only keeps me
from guilty if nigger-lipped pleasures.

They Say They Can Fill Me Up
with a Baby

We have the same President today as yesterday
and what is easier than staying the same?
Teaching Reznikoff I cry and make myself
the spectacle I say most certainly I am not.
Say, *want to be with*, say Buddha
or don't say nothing for which, nothing.
No matter how much it costs to afford
an even million, mother can afford it
yet she does not seem to understand
equivalence, doctoris comma juris et
medicinae doctor and also this other one.
When we talk about literacy there cannot be
one without concessions. Like,
how can this cat have no smell at all?
Something of boxwood and piss must be true
or all childhood was a lie
in the name of bowdlerized peace, black peace.

for Erica Kennedy Johnson

Another bullshit death is an open book
open to the blue-stained vertebrae of boats
which is how a gentleman flips you off

If you think it important when writing
to see-render architectures that count
look Thurston Moore is no more no less
a bad motherfucker than the ugly toe protruding
without grace or being bidden   come
a catchment for some kind of withheld story
that gets told
—a structure *would* withhold to expose itself
If God then secrets   I get that

/

I interrupt my project on siblings
to see the passing of Erica Johnson
far from me   do not even mention it
to my brother who was too young to care
          minor crux   &   perfect "project"
my sister and I speak of her together
in the manner reserved for happenings
at the bedside of a dying person

we shared a lot of Thai food
I learned to go to Barneys in a bad mood
and get some gorgeous blue gloves for the Street
there are three people who know this
one has forgotten one I follow on Twitter
one I maintain is an actual enemy

/

If violence is the unit of joblessness
then bang down your wrist for young mothers
like Emerson covered in concrete
If the man having only just shit his pants
at W4th Street   did the gentlest shuffle
in his own liquid shit
versus my unsullied pants
with the hole large enough for the mosquito
to get in and bite

then what am I reporting here? I am not Wordsworth
this poem begins with the death of Erica Johnson
remembers a man with a book on boats
reflects on how to compose such a poem
on covetousness which might be a sin
returns to blue boats and bespoke
that is its structure

/

a pox of urges
one redraws the face of the aforementioned
gentleman   we wash him with our nipples

if you have not heard your dance music equal
then do not speak if you do not know the Neptunes
stop talking   cut my eye
again   for heaviness
that break a glass dick table

I peek out   separately from Erica Johnson
though the beacon of murmur things
flash me girl

Was a Flat Breast Plate

When everyone was moving to Prague
When everyone was moving to Fort Greene
Was colored and that was complete
Reversal of the circumstance of circumference

Encircled   The circle was of being dispersed
Of trying to live
Was Beckett universe a place
Wasn't no one moving there

Was the bresaola to come with from (not Italy)
The colonial last armored location
Was sliding vertically along the hard
Front of economic history

Was the Starchild of Dawoud Bey, Glenn Ligon & Mickalene Thomas

Regarding sweet milk and hellfire
as passable instances of mimesis
it could be said the takedown
was underway   its long tooth descending
immemorially   when you sit
let it not be with roast beast
nor shall Tropicalia disgrace
twenty pounds of lean muscle
Ali never looked better in shades

Was Old Lion, or,
On the Camino Trail

Lourdes loves a tight high box, a falsetto word, costs very little, is almost free. Lourdes cannot imagine what to do with black leather pants that cost what she costs for four or five years. That is for one pair. Lourdes doesn't care that another person could put them on, but they wouldn't fit. Cat Power's pubes would stand up out of these pants if Richard Avedon were to photograph her from the grave, one day.

It's raw to have no hobbies except chasing objects small enough to pick up and carry in your mouth. Adorno says it is not bourgeois. It is never all that clear whether Adorno is cursing a thing or what, but Lourdes can never be bourgeois or want pants. The form of our togetherness forbids her from spending money. Getting anything, getting freedom or pants, costs money.

Lourdes reminds me of the pilgrims. Gloriana—was dead, a generation of her people sagged into the grave before the action began, perished on the rocks before the evolutionary whoosh of fleet violence. It was Lourdes or them. Choose Lourdes. To worship, to smooth over wrinkles, to light candles, to stroke, to be unable to separate, to walk without water toward, to faint, to be falsely pregnant, and immured, to bite and be bled, to be strait-jacketed, to sanctify, to accidentally kill with fire, to make rich to confound these predators. All this from Lourdes, to her miracle as alleged icon of late maturity.

A Monkey Could do This

at the very first moment in Baltimore there was a thud
it was my great grandmother coming back to earth

(levitate, negro

you could do it just breathe)

up to my chin in what I do not deserve
certainly there is a limit to the utility of Jesus

watch how I am to the touch
flaming off a rifle barrel

wherein I signal inspiration
in wound-up sclera and a ferocious cannonball
toward the rapt attention of the congregants

and raise up in testimony over this here

You and Me are Not Friends, OK?

With "barbecue" in one ear and "chips" in the other, that is how
    a goddess comes
with one calf cramped and a finger up her ass; a goddess comes
    for twenty minutes

only when the seventh record has been turned over, convinced
    that laboring
so closely over your face will kill you in a minute, does she
    relieve herself

with a huffled and casual motherfuck.

The probity of her pussy satisfies all curiosities. "Whatever,
    baby—let's try it."

Doritos might be a distraction but don't be confused about how
    they work: you gotta eat.
I said this. I did this, without pseudonym,

S

At this point, the say back's confused as to sources
a tall Chinese butch at a tacky party
is being admired for neat bigness and a flat chest
before her astonishingly packaged man-junk
in perfect panties I would have chosen for myself
the knock at the door is a polite request to leave
one place that won't deal in prostitution

At this point, return on technology becomes its demise
digital playback can't ring my bell
that cockney bastard stagnates—no, is enveloped
by a curve on The Hana Highway a great deal of rain
some blindness gives up the line that opens "Chelsea"
is being admired for neat bigness and a flat chest
married to another large man in the room

At this point, all language has my bloody stink on it
slavery & mackerel & spoilt cream drag in behind me
a pink thought bubble so thin and dreadful
it threatens the profit of Quentin Tarantino
admired for neat bigness and a flat chest
even as the dog of late reproductive horniness
I would not fuck a man whose death wish

features so prominently the figure of my sister
naked roasting in a box. At this point,
spare me. The penis thematic's comic offenses
overdetermine correct usage not me not you
is capable of parsing a knot what is called love
originary callings for neat bigness and a flat chest
crack the long front of economic history

one each   a dead fish   & a precious blade

balance our several flesh & in our minds

grommeted & unable   words & stars to me

held together by shine held together

outside underwriting nobody

sent us   & sacrifice   folds

attention & cradling the head nun's

plucked bird feelings

the cut matrix   & courage

every time I say something to you

deeply untechnical

sometimes & almost all the time   being cut

clean enough   & served up-

heaven now   & then the gods won't take me

butchered the way we do here

just to be together

the baby   got his lip split open

roughhousing perspective

Preliminary Notes on Street Attacks

I was of three minds
Like a tree
In which there are three blackbirds.

— Wallace Stevens

1 .

pushed out the turnstile by a white man today
being touched in so hostile a manner is better

as against another demonstration of disgust funny
eight thousand times since the age of eleven

when you first got followed down the street
by a stranger trying to grab your boob

you have calculated the nearness
of whosoever is not repelled by your "hostility"

it looks bad to yell at a white man in public
even if he has pushed you out of the way

lie down under the turnstile feign injury
get blood on the perpetrator scratch him

he wants to stand next to a blond girl at a bar
who is not his blond wife right next to him anyway

when a psychotic person is getting on a subway car
and it is impossible to avoid them

I hover near an athletic black man in a suit
tatted-up as long as he is black
no white man on the car would do a thing
if a crazy person with a knife tried to stab you

even take your baby
oh yes they'd let you die

unless you fell on the tracks
as there's some kind of context for that danger

*   *   *

I misunderstand the rules of the supermarket aisle
if I'm thinking sometimes I stare off into space

a white man who imagines he is being eyeballed
can get real crazy but a lady too

told me last week not to roll my eyes at her
a few days after George Zimmerman was acquitted

you could be twenty-three or forty-three
you must cue social status with accessories

my blackface drag
inflected so almost no one

can read it anymore
out   out   out

*   *   *

this white husband my friend says
looks when we are all together in a family like a key

one time some photographers were chasing me
it seemed sure they were going to hurt me

then another time he was at my side
they stood back a respectful distance

he never said nothing to them
sometimes I can get away with cursing a cop

now that I am older and if I am driving a BMW
all my life fancy people think you can be honorary

if you stand near white people
everybody's mood changes

generally not taking shit
when a young black male is getting arrested

stop on the street no matter where you are going
because the watching neighbor

might recognize my child one day
trying to make it back home
Hilton Als wrote in a profile of Kara Walker
of blackness' primal scene

I don't know   punk outside
looking too pretty is technically unproveable

both avoidable and a tangle of ignorance
I don't know much in the way of Benjamin Freud

Marx for twenty years and poorly
in a bubble differentiated from air

only contamination of the gorgeous membrane
swear on this stack of doodoo

on sight I am a unified person

2 .

A nightmare is a dream in which you are in service to a rich woman
of indeterminate ethnicity, forced to walk her thoroughbred
Maine Coon about the City on a leash, for money.

An excellent profiler of need, you are pretty well-suited for
assistance. You recognize the violent misogynist, the narcissist,
the compulsive, the borderline, persons suffering from bipolar
illness, and addicts, immediately.

You thought a poem like this would have a chorus and require
its listeners to hold hands or touch each other on the face,
gently. You thought you'd go for dyspeptic undoing of l'esprit
de l'escalier with classical movement, undo the poem altogether,

but you don't want to be liked for cleverness. You don't want to
touch anyone or be following some girl around a gallery, then bop
her on the head as a blow against racism. The spirit is of lassitude.
You are a glazer.

You like a goddam blackbird and sentences. Inside your head is
a grandiose place. You believe yourself to be above murder, you
don't spit on people. Probably, you think you can learn anything
and explain.

Publicly and for money, you are in service to explanation. One
possible metaphor for microaggression is aphorism. You cannot
come back from explanation to explain the poetry of the poetry.

3 .

Idiot, this morning, every earthly
morning the light smoothness of your life is
unprecedented. A green chicken egg's
color is the problem of being in a shell
on a shelf.
The line to you grows longer, scaled down
by an English witness. You're upset. At a loss
for nettles that never undid the primary illness,
the sensuous thing is unstudied. Not Blake,
nobody.

Come out of that; out of the instanced
listening. In the company of poets, rare spots
afflict the nervous upper lip. Terrific rageful
liar on Whitman on Asphodel, you would lie
to Baraka's face.

Lotion

'I reject an ashy death.'

I came up on some unfamiliar lotion[1] and began to think.

Let us suppose that lotion begins with principles of emulsion, which we know about from food-making. The best lotions are made from what you can eat: fat pressed from the olive and avocado, kernels, seeds and germs of shea, palm, peanut, almond, sunflower, primrose, sunflower, safflower, wheat; even the unlikely peach; even the apricot; the weird oils (o blubber of whale, o America) lanolin and jojoba; fragrant essence of lavender, rose, lemon, sage. When applied to skin in their unprocessed form, any of these, all, naturally, begin to rot.

---

1 This excellent product was manufactured by the company of an old and dear friend, now a successful entrepreneur, among whose ventures include a mini-hair salon set discretely behind a curtain in a shop otherwise devoted to the sale of lotions, shampoos and other beauty products.

Of course, lotion occurs at an intersection of blackness and the market. Lotion and the practices it invokes—simple acts of living such as becoming wet or dry, ingesting or covering oneself in stuff of life—is the undressed and feminine doppelganger of an imaginary space almost completely filled by black music, which dominates every attempt to materialize black imagination. That is, to bring the materially improved self and world into existence.

Lotion proposes roughness, a core condition prone to freaks; it is, in the presence of the corrigible, those who are in need, simulacrum of all the suckings-off the world has ever known.

I do not wash my head everyday unless I have been swimming, which I don't do often as I live in New York and do not swim for exercise. Of a winter's morning when I take off my hat, it is thrilling and also repulsive to perceive a signal odor of black womanhood, rancid oil on the scalp, an odor lodged in memory quite near the smell of lightly singed hair, distinct from the smell of hair and skin chemically burned or "cured" by lye. Anyone who has ever been inside a hair salon frequented by black women knows this trinity of odors. Anyone who has ever been *near* a black woman knows it. (See fn 1.)

Indeed, just the other day, because I care for my own hair and skin, I had taken the unusual step of washing and ironing my hair before beginning an ordinary day of errands, study and writing. Because it was a cold fall day, instead of twisting my hair into a knot and securing it with pins, as is my usual practice on a workday, it occurred to me to rest both hair and scalp by wearing a wool newsboy's cap. Carelessly, I shoved my hair under a hat. A few floppy curls fell out. These I tucked behind my ears. The wind was blowing. I could smell the clean burn of my clean hair on Nostrand Avenue. I could smell it on the A train. It felt good to know that I was capable of caring for my hair and for myself in this way. Loose under my cap, I had coaxed my hair back to health, finally, after submitting to the simple, counter-intuitive truth that it acts better when I keep it straight. This isn't true for everyone, but it is true for me and my particular hair, known in the literature as type 3c (or, it might be 4a). Black hair in its natural state is delicate, and I haven't the time to cultivate mine in the necessary way. I am an intellectual and a woman who must go to work and tend to her own survival. I accept, in my fortieth year, that the work of caring for my natural hair can, at last, be foregone. When I come out of the shower or the sea and people see my hair coiled around my face, they want to know something about why I do not choose this as my default appearance. My sister, my mother and my husband do not ask this silly question; they leave me to my business.

I got to my university and I walked into the ladies room, removing my hat as I entered. A white woman (much older than I am, who should have known better) came out of the john to announce, quite loudly, "Oh my God, what is that smell? Something is burning!" Well, nothing was burning. It was just my hair. Let me remind you that we were in a public toilet where all manner of odors proliferate, the least of which, I think, is the smell of scalded shampoo and protein. "I don't think anything is on fire," I told her, and went into a stall to pee.

My toilette is simple and extremely rigorous. Wash my head once a week. Attend to oral hygiene as frequently as is necessary. (In an age when almost everyone in the City carries some kind of pack, I cannot see why we should not have inside our packs a toothbrush and floss, at the very least. I like to have a little peroxide. My mother taught me this and her mother taught her: hydrogen peroxide for debriding and killing whatever tries to live in the mouth). Pedicures twice a month, never resorting to chemical removal of skin. I keep my fingernails short, and bare. Frequently, I wear no make-up at all, although, if I am feeling old or not very pretty, I resort to a little kohl and gloss. Bathe no less than twice a day. Bathing more frequently than this is a sign of mental illness. Less—for others—is fine.

I remove hair with enormous frequency, but I do not follow the most common or popular practices in this regard. I rarely cut the hair on my head, for example; I find it is unnecessary. Since I keep my hair long, it maintains itself in decent order without the constant trimming many hairstylists recommend. (See fn 1.) In summer, I respect the moderately oppressive governing expectation that I should remove hair under my arms, from my legs, groin and belly. In colder months, I remove hair only as my lover requests, and reluctantly, since I cannot overstate the discomfort and rage I experience each time I subject myself to any variation of the "bikini wax," a barbaric and bizarre practice, the basic point of which (removing hair from the opening of the vagina and around the clitoris) can be accomplished painlessly with a thirty-five dollar pair of electric clippers that serve for years.

Although women speak loudly and publicly of the removal of hair from their labia and ass-cracks, it is considered unseemly to speak of a woman's facial hair outside of a controlled and rigorously policed set of rules. Women and men may speak openly of the practice of shaping a woman's eyebrows. With an intimate, one may speak of removing hair above the upper lip or the removal of a few stray hairs on the chin with a tweezer. Only one woman as hirsute as myself has ever spoken to me of the removal of hair from her neck, from her entire face, in copious amounts from her chin, and she was, herself, a well-compensated expert in these matters, and a black woman, and a beauty. The aestheticians who remove hair from my face play a special role in my life.

The slightly ridiculous bodily conditions each of us lives with daily—after a day of not-writing, the collected and swept up pile of flakes from my cuticles, black oils scraped from beneath my thumbnails, the stray bit of scalp and something swabbed from the cat's eye.

One commercial lotion for my face, one for my body, one for my cuticles and the odd blemish or rash, one for my hands, several for my hair; those I recommend to others, recommendations I have taken. In the refrigerator, ongoing experiments with volatile fats (coconut oil, pure shea); on my bureau emergency lotion purchased while out-of-town, disregarded as useless— wrongly conceived and executed with unreasonably high alcohol or glycerin content. Lotions that are too thin. For years and years, nothing sold over the counter *worked*. For life-long care of simple dry skin, nothing a dermatologist has ever prescribed works. Nothing sold in a department store works. (Occasionally, a wonder like Oil of Olay!) Lotions whose makers choose (wisely) to make a great deal of money instead of excellent lotion. Always, Vaseline, in a pinch. A dab of olive oil is a quick fix.

Lotion is a palliative. What does it correct? It corrects ash. What is ashiness? Ash is a gray track of evident decay, most striking in contrast with darker skins, brown skins, tending to black.

After bathing, I apply both face and body lotions. After handwashing, hand lotion. In the winter, I apply an extra layer of thick oily cream, too oily for the hands (but good for the thin skin on the shins that cracks in cold, dry weather) to my heels and elbows. Sometimes I notice a black woman unknown to me, not homeless, whose legs or feet or hands are so ashy that I wonder whether she has lost her mind.

Liniments are a second class of lotions, meant to address a deeper set of problems.

I find myself on my knees with some rags and a bucket filled with scalding hot soapy water and bleach. My mother has visited and discovered some scuzz on the stepladder that I am obliged to use for retrieving bowls, pitchers and the like from the uppermost shelves in my apartment. I am wiping clots of greasy dirt from the rungs of this already ugly metal thing, scrubbing also the dirty bands of floor that protrude beyond spaces that "cannot be cleaned"—the edge-of-under the refrigerator, the stove, the dishwasher, the poorly installed, cheap formica cabinets. Filth. On my knees now, I perform an act of penitence; in that this dirt has been discovered and named and pointed to, I am humiliated; in that *suggestions* have been made regarding the method of its eradication, too, I am humiliated. Over the telephone, my mother insists that I kneel, of course, on some towels or sheets, folded several times to protect my knees from being scratched or scraped, made dark or scaly from work. "Are you wearing gloves?" she asks. "You wouldn't want to get an infection. It's how your father almost lost his arm. They made him scrub the floors." My father had osteomyelitis as a teenager. A serious infection led to several botched surgeries, all performed while he was locked up in a facility for juveniles somewhere outside Philadelphia. In fights, he used his casts as weapons and never recovered the full use of his scarred right arm and hand. I never knew that, about the floors, I tell my mother, sloshing a rag around in the putrid bucket.

Our crooked fingers are soft, soft, all my parents' children.

I maintain dominion over the crevices of myself, deep into the layers of my skin, which must never be questioned. Never doubt that these crevices extend toward an infinitely receding boundary. Come close to me to feel it.

but pattern is a local feature resonant to the formal field of the whole, and the poem has its formal identity not in itself but in the field of poetry it belongs to

—Robert Duncan

Simone / 11

At dawn the humming has not become so great
as to obstruct inviting inputs of, say, words,
unevenly apportioned at any rate
along, let us call it a pathway, but, if you can,
try not to say "neural," treat condition
as ordnance (what a sound) ordnance, or
tinnitus. If only

       my body would ring like a simple ear.
Draw out an ear with charcoal / whatever they use to draw with
(I don't understand drawing so well, and it's OK. Macro-analyses of
space and color spread my brain tight. They tighten me up, like a
corner, like symphonic gestures, like prosody. Take me outside and
beat me with a fresh green switch
to get that whistling oak twig / holler).
Gross render me an ear.

In possession of my instruments,
slake feeling in the prehensile cool part of day
reading hours away in tribute to 11 occupations.
Originating whole series intakes by reading this way or cracking silent
when they come to rebuild the broken deck.
In the cubby part of day, you would think all capable
of reasoning entire worlds. Transposed coming ray
in evident readiness to talk your way out of the rest.

Michael / 2

for M.P.

I guess I don't have a strong desire / to hear any more Afrobeat
or was over the death of Fela a long time ago, turning now
to Big Black, on watch for Mandela to go over.
Mike Veal, explain this to me; you know the Happy Valley
better than anybody. No one expects the Kingston hostel
kicked-up in perfect salutation of Pinkest queer love
around Independence Day, whichever one.
Musical genius trouble / the fuck out my inner Yankee.

[She. Bet She sun the Devil at Northampton
Gay Head straight his wicked back cane
Pottawatomie. Then left and came back.]

You think a black witch cannot ride frontier light around Leyden,
skip Salem, haunt the Yankee line to straighten
my ragged and beloved East. Pure linearity is Yankee, so the witch
circles out the open sky up there. The broom crosses her jagged
principle effort as counter phenomenon. Broom / joke.
Take my broom. Here. Try to take it.
Make the blacklit Berkshires right now on this humbug,
on this joke sign with a witch on it.

Poem

let us have misprision again everybody
without the technical name for gospel

three creatures in three days bite
against the expected punishments

nothing but mistakes come to mind
that is not a poem I could write

Arthur / 51

for Arthur Miller,

    a handsome man

    in a 'stale' marriage

youthfully proposed in Prospect Park,

tall brown Arthur,

    dark Viking

        full of mashed potatoes

                drunk

ignorant

of the coming

ingénue

Planar

Desire for a clean plane,
measure of lilting planes
of the hands, a sum on the one hand
of two hands and counting feet,
sing muscle.
Muscle scraped, visionary
pectoralis peeled back,
underneath, the heart's minor tapes.

In a clean plane, against
bound breasts, I roll
among permitted variation, I traverse
the gut kept there. Keep to
planes, put away death
inside his thigh.

Kettle to Pot

Unable to pour boiling water
over an edge from kettle to pot
water boils from kettle to neti pot
still boils from kettle to cup running over
boil pool steam pool leak pool

little cooling pot over the boiled edge
of boil pooled salt vapors
sulfurous stank boil heal dangled over
the boiled edge of burnt earth
cooling salt pool nettle stung
black clotted blood at the bottom
of the sink

There was a time I hardly went three steps
Except another black girl was with me.

Mother. Always lonely. I am always.
Mother those girls. Forty-two.

March summer. Light blue. Vermont.
Endless crescent. Invert as a tyke lake.

Fernet Mother. I'm grown. Forest.
San Francisco. Lone cold.

Stone turd. Talk three or none.
Kidding.
Kidding.

Don't nuzzle me fucker-maker
Rinky-dink kale feeding guinea pig
Fonky bag uh cornchips plastic shoe
Wearing crinkle-fry bastard
. . . up in here TONIGHT
Wanchu go head mister plinth butt
And roll ya dumb ass a lavender
Cigarette don't make me slap a freeze
On this wart-o-matic bullshit
Get me a rancorous tinker toy
N turn this motherfucker out

It Must Be Shameless

Apart disclaimed wicked pea, split soft skin
of the principle princess, who writhes,
a little blood passes her perineum every night,
grey linen sheets flax talisman plot luxe
to strip and scrub all gore
a plain bar of secret white soap
it is a pine tree, it is an orange blossom, is it a rose hip
under a baby tongue, blood cuts
punisher, swear it closed, closes it

Probably Your Soulmate

Portland wraps the fruit for export, the remainder left

                  neither _____ nor _____

for birds to bump into. Even the spider has a way

                loves my mother

of stabbing the banana, I guess. The way they are so black

                   the way it is possible to love a fine
                   haughty woman

in the market, the callaloo's so grand and blowsy

                   when everyone knows her husband

so the merchant can reach it from her seat.

              _____

The oily mountain coffee I imagine having tasted as a child

                I must love her then

is nowhere to be found and whoever goes into the bush up the mountain

                   enough for the women who cannot

they can't understand me when I say the darkest what she keeps for herself.

                even when I cannot

I don't know how the sun cooks that turnip transparent

                         tell her, either, anything real

as the Sea; (my family are laughing at me again)

I have no patois for transparent turnip and cannot make myself understood.

Do stop giving me that list; I can't read it.

Anthony

Sat down with Arlo's book today, in which
Jubilee Singers make a map all the time
of the difficult North Star and I try to get easy
enough to make it fair so I can wave at Arlo
maybe sing to you both if I get near enough
alongside friendly-like green-eyed white men

given a reason I could be jealous but never was yet
it's your dancing that specifies the rotation
a nil class position we see in the bafflement of each other
nobody else can get into it like you have become
lost walking away from the original farm

what a relief to be nobody and hold your hand in the middle of the night
when the heat coming from inside me and the klonopin knotted together
are making me real uncomfortable and has been there all this time

Anthony

Sat down with Dana's book today, in which

I had got surprised   every time some photographer
wanted to put me in pictures
begin weeping now   or in the shower over a cystic blemish
aflame in a place you couldn't see before you ran a little more
a little further than you thought you could but not so much your
      toenails fall off
blemish warming in your genes like a tiny fat roll
or shameful tuck of subway muscle behind that weak tendon
but not so weak you can't run any more, love

a surprising number of people more beautiful than average
congregate around my pussy I mean my poverty
ooo see what you made me do, Dana
my heart & lungs are so mean
pound for pound on my feet
the old men in the hood love me as usual
but now I've discovered the blowjob trade
at midday in the chicken joints and candy stores

surprise loathes a feminist come without promises to the corner
sneer to uptight sneer
you know the etymology of uptight, Dana?
not a person who sings to herself not even the soulful music of
      Kenny Gamble

touches the swagger nerve very close to the surface in me
so it's unclear whether she's fucking at this point in time
it's early in the life yet to be written
late in the game though I'm not really sorry

sudden overdevelopment in salutatory surprise
cleans my clock wets my whistle makes the dogs go
mmm girl any day of the week   then let it be every day of the week
fool   Hey, Dana   I think you might be a genius
for the sound of how the street moves through me
on a grosgrain ribbon
the street comes out through every open part of me
do I or do I not keep it in my pants

Anthony

Sat down with Anselm's book today, in which
Obviously drunk my favorite secret is how quietly drunk I can be
I spread my toes over the silken surface of GQ
So little lights come on in the wordspace
Plinky lights shaped like chili peppers
Memorialize the skinny drunk phase of life
Where my record of arrest and recovery's absolutely pristine
When I could no longer drink bourbon I stole dyed beaver
I wrested gauze kimono from racist manners
I called the cops myself
Stationed under the aqueduct
The eighteenth century blows in on the creek wind and stinks of
plain black dirt
Some horseshit mixed in for good measure
Yes, I was coming up the street home
And a white guy on a horse traveled with me for a while
He talked to me about his family stables
Like in Philadelphia sometimes happens because it ain't New York

THANKS

Aracelis Girmay, Stefania Heim, erica kaufman, Anna Moschovakis, Imani Perry, Litia Perta, Joy Phillips, Lorrin Thomas, Cheryl Jones-Walker, Santi White, Hope Wilson: forever. Anselm Berrigan, Erica Hunt, Eileen Myles: corner. Anthony Leslie: Isaac. The Poetry Project: crew. Jerry Gafio Watts: missing piece.

To the editors of these publications where some of these poems originally appeared: *The Baffler*, *Big Bell*, *boundary2*, *The Brooklyn Rail*, *The Claudius App*, *Critical Quarterly*, *Epiphany* and *Washington Square*.